D0537346

Communities

Living in a Desert

By Jan Kottke

Welcome
Books

Children's Press

A Division of Scholastic Inc.
New York • Toronto • London • Auckland • Sydney
Danbury, Connecticut

Photo Credits: p. 5, 7, 9, 11, 13, 15 © National Geographic Image Collection; p. 17, 19, 21 © Index Stock Imagery
Contributing Editor: Jennifer Ceaser
Book Design: MaryJane Wojciechowski

Visit Children's Press on the Internet at:
http://publishing.grolier.com

Cataloging-in-Publication Data

Kottke, Jan
    Living in a desert / by Jan Kottke.
      p. cm.—(Communities)
    Includes bibliographical references and index.
    Summary: Three children describe their lives in the Sahara,
the Gobi, and the Syrian deserts.
    ISBN 0-516-23300-9 (lib. bdg.)—ISBN 0-516-23500-1 (pbk.)
    1.   Desert people—Juvenile literature   2.   Deserts—
Juvenile literature   [1.   Desert people   2.   Deserts]
    I.   Title   II.   Series
2000
    577.54—dc21

Contents

My name is Hala (**ha**-la).

The Syrian (**syr**-ee-ahn) **desert** is my home.

My donkey helps me carry water from the **well**.

This is my brother, Abbas
(a-**bas**).

Behind him is our house.

Our house is made of rocks.

7

My mother and my aunts make bread.

My mother pushes the bread flat.

Aunt Mina (**mee**-nah) cooks the flat bread over a fire.

9

My name is Tarik (**tah**-reek).

The Sahara (se-**hayr**-ah) desert is my home.

I help my father **herd** our sheep.

11

We have a house made of stone.

We also have a camel.

13

These are boys from my **village**.

They are herding their animals along the **sandy** road.

15

My name is Batu (**bah**-too).

The Gobi (**go**-be) desert is my home.

17

This is a **ger** (**gur**).

It is where I live with my family.

A ger is a round house made of cloth.

19

This is my mother and father.

They are returning from the city.

Our donkey pulls a cart full of food.

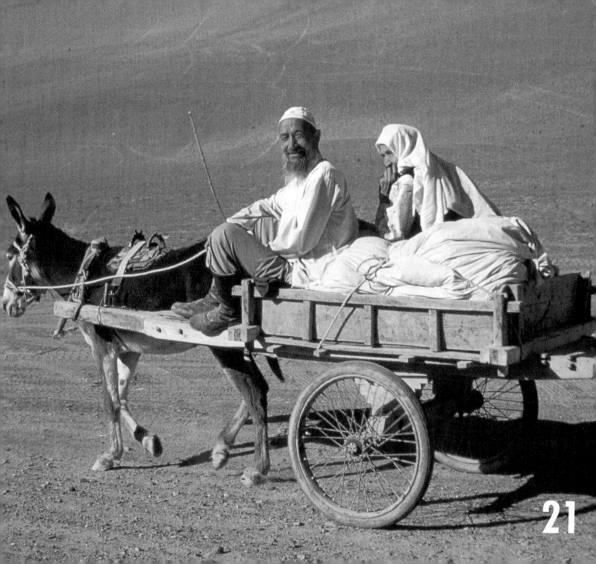
21

New Words

desert (**dez**-urt) a dry place with a lot
of sand and little water

ger (**gur**) a round house made of cloth

herd (**hurd**) to show a group of
animals the way

sandy (**san**-dee) covered with sand

village (**vil**-ij) a group of houses where
people live; a small town

well (**wel**) a hole dug in the ground to
get water

To Find Out More

Books
Ali, Child of the Desert
by Jonathan London and Ted Lewin
Lothrop, Lee & Shepard Books

Cactus Desert
by Donald M. Silver and Patricia J. Wynne
W.H. Freeman & Company

Living in a Desert
by Alan Fowler
Children's Press

Web Site
On the Line—Deserts
http://www.ontheline.org.uk/explore/nature/deserts/deserts.htm
Has information about deserts, including animal life, plant life,
and weather.

Index

About the Author
Jan Kottke is the owner/director of several preschools in the Tidewater area of Virginia. A lifelong early education professional, she is completing a phonics reading series for preschoolers.

Reading Consultants
Kris Flynn, Coordinator, Small School District Literacy, The San Diego County Office of Education

Shelly Forys, Certified Reading Recovery Specialist, W.J. Sahnow Elementary School, Waterloo, IL

Peggy McNamara, Professor, Bank Street College of Education, Reading and Literacy Program